The Lost Gospel

Q

The Lost Gospel

Q

The Original Sayings of Jesus

CONSULTING EDITOR
Marcus Borg

INTRODUCTION
Thomas Moore

EDITORS
Mark Powelson   Ray Riegert

Seastone

BERKELEY, CALIFORNIA

Published by:
Seastone, an imprint of Ulysses Press
P.O. Box 3440
Berkeley, CA 94703
www.ulyssespress.com

Library of Congress has cataloged the hardcover version of this book as follows:

Library of Congress Cataloging-in-Publication Data
The lost gospel Q: the original sayings of Jesus / consulting editor, Marcus Borg : introduction, Thomas Moore : editors, Mark Powelson, Ray Riegert.
p. cm.
Includes bibliographical references.
ISBN 1-56975-100-5 (hardcover)
1. Q hypothesis (Synoptics criticism)
I. Borg, Marcus J. II. Powelson, Mark. III. Riegert, Ray.
BS2555.2.L66 1996
226'.066--dc20

96-35241 CIP

ISBN 1-56975-189-7 (paperback)

Printed in Canada by Transcontinental Printing

10 9 8 7 6 5 4

Cover Design: Big Fish
Interior Design: Sarah Levin Design

Distributed in the United States by Publishers Group West and in Canada by Raincoast Books.

For Bev and Ted
Marcus Borg

To my mother and father
Mark Powelson

For GG and Gib
Ray Riegert

Contents

Introduction

by Thomas Moore

The haunting, inspiring and challenging words of Jesus have now been with us for two thousand years. During all that time they have been used to moralize, instruct, defend and condemn as well as to lead and guide. As scholars have pointed out for over a century, the four Gospels are riddled with the interpretations, biases and agendas of their editors. Amid the clutter of age-old conflicting readings, it often seems difficult to hear an original voice and to take to heart the wisdom of one of the world's greatest teachers.

The Lost Gospel Q, the scholars' best attempt to render the pure voice of the Gospel Jesus, offers us an extraordinary opportunity to approach with an open mind, fresh ears and new understanding the good news of the mysterious kingdom that Jesus announced. Reading these simple but puzzling words is like sitting in the presence of a teacher. Here we have the opportunity to listen actively and individually to a real voice, to catch the nuances and perceive the personality.

For many who are familiar with the language of the Gospels, it could be an eye-opening revelation to read the sayings of Jesus without the usual contextualization of his words. A reader might discover wisdom instead of moralizing, beauty and poetry rather than opinion and unfathomable mystery instead of plain persuasion. Q offers us a glimpse of the Gospel's soul and not merely its message.

The effort to make a religious or spiritual life can sometimes get bogged down in questions that fail to get to the heart of the matter: Who is right? What are the facts? What is the proper way to live? The great literature of the world's religions reaches so deep into the nature of things that such questions are revealed as too shallow. By being in touch with the depths of one's soul, by realizing the absolute communal nature of human life, and by being open fearlessly to the mystery at the base of human life a person will find far deeper resources for an ethical life than from a list of minimal moral standards. Attending church and professing belief, though valuable routes to a spiritual life, may not be sufficient to create a true appreciation of sacredness. We need words of exceptional power and mystery to lead us beyond our own agendas and understandings.

The sayings of Jesus that we find in The Lost Gospel Q address the mystery directly. They read like the sacred poetry of the Old Testament and of other religious traditions. They generate religious wonder rather than simple notions of divinity and faith. They challenge a reader toward deeper reflection on the human situation, and they invert familiar values.

The urge to discover in a scientific manner the historical Jesus and his own words has its place, but history is always changing as historians move in and out of vogue with their various theories and approaches. The fantasy of origins, the sense of being in the presence of an authentic and primary text, accomplishes something of importance. It focuses the imagination in a special way, inclining the reader toward a pure, open-minded approach to thoughts and images that may have become too familiar.

Stripped of many details of setting and purpose, the words of the Lost Gospel Q reach deeper in the imagination—a key factor in the relation between a sacred text and its readers. It is easy to read any holy text too lightly or assume too much about its meaning and intention. Our very notion of the spiritual life deepens as we allow sacred stories and sayings to penetrate that part of us that is free of our own agendas and habits of thought.

The sayings in Q ask us to turn conventional wisdom upside down. Spiced with paradox, irony and wit, they move our reflections in unusual directions. Psychologically, they shift our attention from the structures that provide us with conventional and comfortable meaning to more challenging and fruitful reconsiderations and revisions. In this way, they offer new life and vitality.

I will place this beautiful, well-presented book with its excellent translation among my few primary resources from the world's religious and spiritual literature. I will read it differently than I do other books, treating it as one of the primary revelations of life's sacredness. I expect it to give me a Jesus who is less shielded and packaged by later traditions, less nuanced by the purposes of well-intentioned institutions, and therefore more poetic and more sublimely relevant to my own desire for a truly intelligent, deeply felt and socially responsive life of spirit.

Preface

by Marcus Borg, Ph.D.

It is an honor and a pleasure to write a preface to this edition of The Lost Gospel Q, one deliberately designed to make Q available to the general reading public.

The Lost Gospel Q is of great interest and importance because, in the judgment of most scholars, it is the first Christian Gospel.

Written in the 50s of the first century, only a couple of decades after the death of Jesus, Q is significantly earlier than the four Gospels of the New Testament. Mark, the earliest of these, was written around the year 70; Matthew and Luke followed a decade or two later; and John probably in the last decade of the first century.

Only the genuine writings of Paul, most of which were also written in the 50s, are as early as Q. But his writings were not Gospels, but letters. They were his personal and pastoral correspondence with early Christian communities outside the Jewish homeland and addressed issues facing those communities. Paul's letters thus contain very little material about Jesus as a figure of history, his teachings and deeds; that was not their purpose. Therefore Q is not only the first Christian Gospel, but the earliest written form of the Jesus tradition.

In the last twenty-five years, Q has been one of the hot spots of the historical study of the Gospels and Jesus, a major focal point of scholarly research. In North America, this work is associated especially with James Robinson, Arland Jacobson, John Kloppenborg, Burton Mack and Leif Vaage.

Yet the claim that there was a Lost Gospel Q—that is, an early Christian collection of the sayings of Jesus, older than all of the surviving Gospels—is not a recent innovation. The scholarly case for the existence of Q was first made over one hundred fifty years ago. By the early 1900s, Q had become widely accepted by scholars involved in the study of Christian origins.

The basis for the "Q hypothesis," as it is commonly called, is a large amount of material (over two hundred verses) found in both Matthew and Luke, but not in Mark. Most scholars do not think that either the author of Matthew or the author of Luke knew the other's Gospel. Therefore the material they share in common cannot be the result of one borrowing from the other, but must come from an earlier written source to which they both had access. That common source was the Lost Gospel Q.

Thus Q is a hypothetical document; no copy of it has ever been found. It is therefore possible to deny that it existed, and some scholars do not accept the Q hypothesis. But most do. My impression is that at least 90 percent of contemporary Gospel scholars do. It seems to them (and to me) a necessary hypothesis.

So, accepting the highly probable hypothesis that Q existed, what was it like? Q was a sayings Gospel. It consists primarily of sayings attributed to Jesus, and some to his contemporary and mentor John the Baptist. To make the point negatively, Q contains very few stories about Jesus. Unlike the Gospels of the New Testament, Q is not a narrative Gospel. There are no birth stories, no death and resurrection stories. There are almost no miracle stories. The one exception (the healing of a centurion's servant) has as its climax a saying of Jesus, so even the exception fits the basic pattern of Q as a sayings Gospel.

These sayings fall into three main categories. The largest category is wisdom teaching—sayings about how to live "the way" that Jesus taught. A somewhat smaller category consists of conflict and judgment sayings. The former includes sayings in which Jesus criticized practices and/or groups that were part of his social world, or in which he responded to criticisms directed against him. The latter threatened a coming judgment by God. It should be noted that judgment in the biblical tradition does not necessarily mean "the last judgment"; the prophets of the Hebrew Bible most often spoke of God's judgment as happening within history rather than bringing history to a close. The third and smallest category consists of teachings about Jesus himself: his temptations by Satan and his responses, and his saying about his relationship to God being like that of son to father.

The presence of these somewhat diverse categories of material is among the reasons for a recent development in Q studies. Namely, beginning in the mid-1980s, some scholars argued that Q can be separated into three layers or stages of development; to put the point only slightly differently, that Q went through three editions or redactions. These successive layers or editions are designated Q^1, Q^2 and Q^3.

Q^1—the wisdom material—is seen as the earliest (probably put into writing in the 50s) and closest to what Jesus himself taught. Though demanding, Q^1 is essentially optimistic and reflects the enthusiasm of the early years of the Jesus movement. Q^2, with its elements of conflict and judgment, reflects a later stage in the movement's history, during which opposition to and rejection of the movement had become pronounced (the 50s and perhaps early 60s of the first century). Q^3 is slightly later, and reflects the movement's emerging christological beliefs about Jesus as the son of God.

But many scholars are skeptical that Q can be divided into successive layers of development. The issue is not whether Q was a developing tradition; clearly it was, just as the Gospels as a whole are the product of the developing traditions of early Christian movements. The issue, rather, is whether Q can be neatly divided into a series of discernible and discrete stages of development. The present volume does not divide Q into Q^1, Q^2 and Q^3, but presents it as an integrated whole.

Like all the Gospels, the Lost Gospel Q can be read on two different levels. That is, it can be read with two different questions in mind. Both are very interesting and centrally important for the study of Jesus and Christian origins. First, what does it tell us about the people in the community who produced it? What does it disclose about their situation, convictions and practices, their vision of life and sense of what was most central, their beliefs about Jesus? Second, what does it suggest about Jesus as a historical figure? Here the focus is not on the community itself, but on the way in which the document functions as a lens for glimpsing the historical Jesus.

I do not wish to suggest comprehensive answers to these questions in this preface. It would be impossible to do so; moreover, the purpose of the questions is to guide your own reading of the Lost Gospel Q. But I do wish to make a couple of remarks.

I begin with the most striking thing the Lost Gospel Q tells us about the community that produced it. On the assumption that Q contains what was most central to the Q community, it provides evidence for an early Christian community that did not make the death and resurrection of Jesus central to its message. Q contains no passion narrative, no death and resurrection stories. It is an important point. For this community, what mattered most about Jesus was not his death and resurrection; the community did not stress "believing" that Jesus "died for our sins and rose again."

What did matter for the Q community was the teaching of Jesus. To a large extent Q is a classic "Two Ways" teaching, a form known in the Jewish tradition and in most religions. There is the wise way and the foolish way, the narrow way and the broad way. One way leads to life, the other to death. The sayings in Q most often speak of the way or path that Jesus taught, a way deeply subversive of the dominant cultural consciousness of his day, and perhaps of every day. Here was a form of early Christianity (probably Galilean) that centrally emphasized "The Way," to use the phrase cited in the Book of Acts as the earliest name for the Christian movement. It is quite different from most traditional and modern forms of Christianity.

Yet too much should not be made of this point. For example, though it means that the theology of the Q Christians was quite different from the theology of Paul, the two points of view do not seem to me to be intrinsically irreconcilable.

Of course, the Lost Gospel Q tells us much more about the Q community, but I leave that to your reading. I turn now to the second question: What glimpses does Q have of Jesus? A caution: Just because the Lost Gospel Q is relatively early, we should not think of it as a near transcript of events and teachings going back to Jesus himself. As noted earlier, Q is the product of a developing tradition, and some of the material in it is unlikely to go back to Jesus. With that caution in mind, what picture of Jesus emerges?

Taking Q as a whole, I will mention six elements. First, Jesus was a wisdom teacher with a metaphoric mind—a teacher of an unconventional wisdom, commonly expressed in memorable aphorisms. He was a master of the one-liner.

Second, he was a radical cultural critic. Though subversion of cultural consciousness is characteristic of most teachers of unconventional wisdom, there is also sharp and passionate social criticism in Q. It is directed against wealth and against the ruling elites (religious, political and economic); indeed, the Jesus of Q threatens Jerusalem (the home of the elites) with divine judgment. The social passion of Jesus' radical cultural criticism makes him similar to the great social prophets of the Hebrew Bible. Third, from Q we would discern that Jesus was a religious ecstatic. He had visions, undertook a wilderness ordeal or vision quest, spent long hours in prayer, was said by his critics to be spirit-possessed, and spoke of God with intimate metaphors.

Fourth, we would surmise that he was a healer and exorcist. Though Q has only one healing story, it contains sayings about both healings and exorcisms. Fifth, the Q community spoke of Jesus as the Wisdom of God (that is, as the Sophia of God), and as the Son of God (though not yet in an ontological sense). Whether either christological image goes back to Jesus is much-debated and uncertain. Sixth, the Jesus of Q spoke of both an apocalyptic eschatology and a sapiential eschatology. The former speaks of a supernatural intervention by God coming in the imminent future; it stresses waiting for God to act, as the contemporary Jesus scholar John Dominic Crossan puts it. The second speaks of the ending of the world of cultural consciousness and domination brought about through response to an enlightened teacher. To echo Crossan again, the second form stresses that God is waiting for us to act. Both are in Q; whether both can be traced back to Jesus (and if so, how they are qualified by each other) is another question.

Like all editions of the Lost Gospel Q, the present one is a reconstruction from non-Markan material shared in common by Matthew and Luke. Mark Powelson and Ray Riegert, the editors of this volume, have immersed themselves in the history of Q scholarship from the nineteenth century to the present, and are thoroughly conversant with the recent burst of publishing on Q. Their reconstruction largely follows the order of Q as found in John Kloppenborg's recent foundational study. They have made major use of massive commentaries by W. D. Davies and Dale Allison (on Matthew) and Joseph Fitzmyer (on Luke). They have considered the conclusions of scholars from the more conservative end of the scholarly spectrum, such as I. Howard Marshall and Robert Guelich. Their translation takes into account multiple versions of the Bible, even as it is also often fresh. I commend this volume to you, and I invite you to explore for yourself the earliest layer of the Jesus tradition.

The Lost Gospel

Q

The Story of the Lost Gospel Q

During the decades immediately following the death of Jesus, small bands of believers wandered the countryside around Galilee. Many were poor people—barefoot, sparsely clothed, lacking staffs and bags—who traveled from village to village. Their homeland was a region of loamy farms and straw-colored hills. The larger towns were linked by Roman roads cobbled with a chalky stone that blew into white dust clouds as the pilgrims passed.

Some spoke like prophets. Others were charismatics who seemed to the uninitiated to hover somewhere between a position of grace and a state of madness. Many were simple folk who sought out friendly houses that would share a meal along the way. Like other first-century Galileans, some of the men had long, ringleted hair and wore rectangular cloaks that were draped across the body. They were bearded and spoke in the soft, slurred syllables of the Aramaic tongue. Women were clad in more colorful garments, which they sometimes belted with a sash.

They were Jews. Most had grown up within a hundred miles of the magnificent temple in Jerusalem, the center of Judaism in the Roman world. But to many this holy spot was less a place of pilgrimage than an urban center of the ruling elite. These were the farmers and fishermen, the homeless and afflicted whom Jesus had called "the salt of the earth."

Unknowingly, they were creating a new sect within Judaism that would soon blossom into a religion of its own. The laws of ritual purity and temple sacrifice practiced in Jerusalem were less important than Jesus' ideas of sharing with the impure and dispossessed. They believed that a new age was approaching, one that called for a revolutionary change of heart. Giving up worldly possessions and following a simple lifestyle would bring them closer to God than listening to the high priests. What these Mediterranean peasants had in mind was a new world in which God's presence could be felt on earth by even the simplest people, regardless of their status and background. They were among the first Christians.

Their beliefs were derived from Jesus' teachings and were contained in a collection of his sayings. Passed along orally at first, these quotes eventually were recorded in written form, the Lost Gospel Q.

Whereas Jewish scribes had been recording holy text on long scrolls for centuries, the Lost Gospel Q was possibly a codex, a forerunner to the modern-day book. Codices were made by chopping papyrus sheets into rectangles and then stacking them. Holes were punched along the side, loose-leaf style, and the manuscript was bound together by leather thongs and covered with wood or animal hide. The result was a primitive book slightly larger than the one you are holding. Whereas scrolls were created by scribes practiced in the art of calligraphy, early codices were copied by workaday hands. More functional than precious, the codex was a handbook, a portable text suited to the wandering missionary.

Crude as it was, this sayings Gospel presented the original version of some of Jesus' most profound teachings. Here was the Sermon on the Mount and the Lord's Prayer, the story of John the Baptist and the parable of the lost sheep. It contained aphorisms and advice and offered guidance on living a compassionate life. Unlike the books of Matthew, Mark, Luke and John that would follow during the next several decades, the Lost Gospel Q lacked narrative and did not mention Jesus' birth or death. It was his teachings, not his crucifixion, that were important.

This first Gospel was compiled by some of the earliest followers in his native Galilee. Written about two decades after Jesus' death, it is older than the traditional Gospels, older than the Christian church itself. Q, quite simply, is the closest we can come to the historical Jesus. More than any other document, this text holds the answer to the mysteries surrounding Jesus.

But no copy of it has ever been found. The words of Jesus you are about to read were not deciphered by archaeologists from the leaves of a crumbling manuscript. Rather than a single rare find, the discovery of the Lost Gospel Q has been the result of over one hundred fifty years of detective work by historians and theologians. They did not disinter it from archaeological layers of earth, but found it buried within the literary layers of the New Testament itself.

The solution to the mystery of the Lost Gospel Q began in Germany during the 1830s. Probing into the synoptic Gospels, historians began discovering unusual patterns in the texts. It seemed that the authors of Matthew and Luke had copied heavily from the Book of Mark. This meant that contrary to centuries of church tradition, which had accorded Matthew the primary position, Mark was actually the first of the four Gospels. Then in 1838, Christian Weisse, a lecturer in philosophy and theology at the University of Leipzig, unearthed proof that Matthew and Luke had drawn not only from the Book of Mark, but from a second source as well.

Laying the books of Matthew and Luke side by side, Weisse realized that this unknown second source was filled with sayings of Jesus that did not appear in the Book of Mark. It soon became known as "Q," drawing its name from the German word "Quelle" or "source." Ironically, it took another hundred years and the archaeological discovery of a different document to fully substantiate Weisse's theory.

It was December 1945, just a few months after the end of World War II, when a treasure trove of early Christian manuscripts was discovered along the Upper Nile River in a town called Nag Hammadi. Unlike the Dead Sea Scrolls, unearthed just a few years later, these documents were codices covered in leather and containing Christian writings.

Among the thirteen precious books was one very unusual volume that triggered a revolution in Bible studies, the impact of which is still being felt. It was called the Gospel of Thomas and consisted of 114 sayings purportedly spoken by the "Living Jesus." Here was an unknown Gospel similar in form and content to the document implied in Weisse's findings. Like Q, the Gospel of Thomas did not mention the birth or death of Jesus. Most significant of all, over one-third of the sayings it contained were similar to those in the Lost Gospel Q!

This indicated that Q was more than a collection of quotes. Like the Gospel of Thomas, it was a Gospel, a vital handbook for early Christians. Then during the 1980s, biblical historian John Kloppenborg demonstrated that collections of wisdom sayings similar to the Lost Gospel Q had served as instruction books during the time of Jesus. Scholars from around the world, finally realizing the importance of this first Gospel, formed the International Q Project and the Q Project of the Society of Biblical Literature to spearhead further investigations into what had proved to be the original source for over two hundred twenty-five verses in the books of Matthew and Luke.

By extracting Q from the pages of the traditional Gospels, historians have uncovered a missing link between Judaism and Christianity. In a sense, the Lost Gospel Q is pre-Christian. It was later writers who added the details about Jesus' life and death that became the bedrock of

Christian belief. Jesus in the Lost Gospel Q is neither Christ nor the Messiah but rather the last in a long line of Jewish prophets. He is a charismatic teacher, a healer, a simple man filled with the spirit of God. Jesus is also a sage, the personification of Wisdom, cast in the tradition of King Solomon.

Synagogues in Galilee were not temples but meeting places, town halls where Jews gathered to sing, pray, gossip and debate scripture. People in Jesus' time would have sat on the benches that lined every wall and listened as he rose, moved to the center of the small room and began to speak. His words were probably very similar to the message that lies within Q.

Jesus talks about villages, neighbors, spouses and children. There are lessons on the relation between households, borrowing and the importance of helping one another. The passages he quotes from the Old Testament are part of a popular tradition, simple sayings that do not reflect a learned interpretation. His imagery is rural and agricultural, creating a portrait of Galilee with its mud huts, tilled fields and fishing villages.

Most important to the destitute people who surrounded Jesus, there is a vision of the future. He speaks in Q of a new age and a higher form of happiness, and calls upon his listeners to follow, even when that means breaking family ties and sacrificing possessions. It is everyone's responsibility to bring this new age, this realm of God, into being. The realm, in turn, is open to everyone regardless of their status, background or ability. In the parable of the supper, those originally invited end up on the outside looking in, while homeless people living along alleyways and country roads enjoy the feast.

The Lost Gospel Q is a guidebook to the land of the soul. It provides simple advice on getting along in the world. There are instructions on the everyday and the eternal alike. The message to each individual is that he or she is important, vital in fact, part of the fabric of the world. In stressing the individual, it turns the imperial Roman world of the first century upside down, proclaiming that, "The last will be first and the first will be last."

What then happened to this text? Why has it been missing for two millennia? Why isn't it part of the New Testament? One very obvious answer is that when the authors of Matthew and Luke wrote their texts, they combined the Lost Gospel Q with the story of the birth in Bethlehem and Jesus' ministry in Galilee and beyond. Then, in one of the most moving passages in literature, they recounted his arrest in the holy city, the subsequent trials before high priests and Roman officials and his execution.

Simply stated, Matthew and Luke were more complete. Their texts could have eventually replaced the earlier Gospel. Also noteworthy is the importance they accorded to the apostles. Barely mentioned in the Lost Gospel Q, the twelve disciples are portrayed in the traditional Gospels as the rightful heirs of Christ's kingdom. His earthly power is passed along to them in what has become known as the apostolic succession, a tradition that even today places the Pope in a direct line of spiritual descent from Jesus. It was the early church fathers who helped to determine the canon of the New Testament, and in doing so they would have been concerned about the role of the disciples in any text.

Strange too is the failure of modern-day scholars to unveil the Lost Gospel Q before the general public. Whereas large sections of the Dead Sea Scrolls were willfully withheld from the world for over forty years by a small group of academics, Q has been endlessly debated by scholars who seem more concerned with the precise shape and wording of the document than in presenting it to the public. They have provided translations of the text but, ironically, have buried them in lengthy treatises much as the text once lay hidden in the books of Matthew and Luke.

Their sin has been one of omission rather than commission. But now it is time, as the quest for the historical Jesus increasingly becomes a matter of public interest and spiritual concern, for everyone to have access to his earliest teachings. Q is, after all, both a doorway into the world of ancient Christianity and a window onto the soul and spirit of Jesus. What we have is a long-lost gospel with a very contemporary message.

THESE ARE THE SAYINGS of Jesus.

Q1 IN THOSE DAYS THE word of God came to John
the Baptist, the son of Zechariah, in the desert of
Judea. He went throughout the Jordan area, calling
for baptism and a change of heart leading to the
forgiveness of sins. As it is said in the book of the
prophet Isaiah,

"A voice cries out in the desert:

Prepare a way for the Lord, clear a straight path for him."

Anyone who has heard the expression "Repent, for the kingdom of God is at hand!" is familiar with the Greek word *metanoia*. Here it is translated to signify a profound "change of heart" or "change of mind," a transformation in goals and life direction. But for centuries, the term has implied the Christian concepts of good and evil and has been translated as "repentance" or "conversion."

CROWDS CAME FROM JERUSALEM and Judea Q2
and the regions around the Jordan River to be baptized by John. He said to them, "Brood of vipers, who warned you to flee from the impending doom? Produce good fruit. Prove that your hearts are really changed. Do not think of saying to yourselves, 'We are Abraham's children' because, I tell you, God can produce children for Abraham right out of these rocks. Even now the axe is aimed at the roots of the trees, so that any tree that fails to produce good fruit will be cut down and thrown on the fire."

The crowds asked him, "So what shall we do?"

He answered them, "Whoever has two shirts must share with someone who has none. Whoever has food should do the same."

Q3 EVEN TAX COLLECTORS CAME to be baptized, and asked John, "Teacher, what shall we do?"

He answered them, "Charge no more than the official rate."

Soldiers also asked him, "And what about us?"

He replied, "Don't harass people. No more extortion. Be satisfied with your pay."

No contemporary word can capture the emotional impact that the term "tax collector" had on people in Jesus' time. To support the largest empire the world had ever known, Rome imposed over fifty different taxes and levies in places like Galilee. To collect, Roman officials often hired unscrupulous brokers who squeezed as much money as possible from an angry populace.

John the Baptist said, "I baptize you with water, but someone more powerful than me is coming. I am not fit to untie his sandals. He will baptize you with holy spirit and fire. His pitchfork is in his hand, ready to thresh the grain. He will gather the wheat into his granary; but he will burn the chaff in a fire that never goes out." Q4

Although they are its major practitioners today, Christians did not initiate the ceremony of baptism. It is an ancient rite dating back to the Egyptians and the mystery cults. Most Jews no longer practice this ritual bathing, but many did in Jesus' time. In fact, the excavations at Qumran that produced the Dead Sea Scrolls also revealed an important immersion site.

Q5 JESUS CAME FROM GALILEE to the Jordan River to be baptized by John. After Jesus was baptized, he prayed and the sky opened up. The holy spirit came to him as a dove, and a voice came from the sky saying, "You are my son. Today I have become your father."

FILLED WITH THE HOLY spirit, Jesus left the Jordan and was guided into the wilderness. Here he was put to the test by the devil for forty days. During that time he fasted and when it was over he was very hungry. Then the devil said to him, "If you are God's son, turn this stone into a loaf of bread." But Jesus replied, "Scripture says: 'People cannot live on bread alone.' " ϙ6

Visitors to modern-day Israel will still find a sun-scorched region of sharp limestone cliffs and wind-blown dust stretching southeast from Jerusalem to the Dead Sea. Known in Hebrew as Jeshimon or "the Devastation," this was the wilderness that Jesus entered.

Q7 THEN THE DEVIL TOOK Jesus to Jerusalem and made him stand at the top of the Temple. "To prove you are God's son," he said to him, "jump down from here. And remember, it is written:

'He will send his angels to guard you and to catch you in their hands so you won't even hit your foot on a stone.' "

Jesus answered him, "It has been said:
'You must not put God to the test.' "

Sitting atop an enormous complex that covered nearly thirty-five acres, the temple in Jerusalem was entered through monumental marble gates. The great Jewish historian Josephus, who lived a generation after Jesus, said that if you climbed to the top of the tower, "you would become dizzy and couldn't even see the end of the measureless depth before you."

THEN TAKING HIM TO a high mountain, the Q8
devil showed Jesus in an instant all the empires of the world. "I will give you the power and glory of these kingdoms, for it is mine, and I can give it to anyone I want. All you have to do is worship me."

Jesus retorted, "It is written:

'You must worship God and serve him alone.' "

Having exhausted all these ways of tempting Jesus, the devil left him, to return at a later time.

One of the Greek words in this passage is *oikoumene*, which literally means "all the inhabited world" and was commonly used to refer to the Roman Empire. The devil, it seems, is tempting Jesus with the earthly power of an emperor.

Q9 AROUND THIS TIME, JESUS went out into the hills seeking solitude and spent the entire night in prayer. At daybreak, he came down with his disciples.

A great crowd of people from all parts of Judea, Jerusalem and the coastal region of Tyre and Sidon had come to hear him and be cured of their diseases.

Fixing his eyes on his disciples he began to speak: "Fortunate are you who are poor, for yours is the realm of God."

"Prayer" in ancient Palestine usually meant the recitation of long set prayers, often proclaimed aloud and in public. In retreating to the hills for long hours of solitude, Jesus was probably engaged in what today we would call meditation.

HAPPY ARE YOU WHO are hungry now, you shall be satisfied. Q10

Fortunate are you who weep now, for you shall laugh.

Known as the Beatitudes, these sayings traditionally have been translated with the expression "blessed are." Actually, the Greek word is makarios, whose rich meaning includes "congratulations to," "happy is" and "fortunate are."

Q11 FORTUNATE ARE THE GENTLE,
for they shall inherit the earth.

The most famous passage in this Sermon on the Mount has always been translated as "the meek shall inherit the earth." Actually, the Greek word praotes means "gentle but strong" and connotes strength that is under control and tinged with a spirit of caring.

HAPPY ARE THE MERCIFUL, for they shall be shown mercy. Q12

Happy are the pure in heart, for they shall see the face of God.

Fortunate are the peacemakers, for they shall be called sons of God.

Q13 FORTUNATE ARE YOU WHEN people hate you, exclude you, abuse you and denounce you on my account.

Celebrate when that day comes and dance for joy—your reward will be great in heaven. Remember that their ancestors treated the prophets this way.

LOVE YOUR ENEMIES. Q14

Do good to those who hate you.

Bless those who curse you.

Pray for those who treat you badly.

The idea of loving your enemies rather than retaliating against them was as radical in Jesus' time as it is today. As one ancient Greek thinker put it, "I consider it established that one should do harm to one's enemies and be of service to one's friends."

Q15 WHEN SOMEONE STRIKES YOU on the right cheek, offer them the other cheek, too.

When someone takes your coat from you, let them have your shirt as well.

Give to everyone who asks. And if someone robs you, don't demand your property back.

To strike someone on the right cheek usually meant striking them with the back of the hand. In Middle Eastern culture, this was twice as insulting as a slap delivered with the palm of the hand.

TREAT PEOPLE AS YOU would like them to treat you. Q16

If you love those who love you, what credit is that to you? Even sinners do the same. If you do good only to those who do good to you, what merit is there in that? Even sinners do that. And if you lend to those from whom you hope to receive, what reward is there in that? Even sinners lend to sinners.

Instead, love your enemies and do good, expecting nothing in return. You will have a great reward, and you will be children of your Father in heaven. He makes the sun rise on the bad and the good. He sends rain to fall on both the just and the unjust.

The original Hebrew word translated as "to sin" in the Bible actually meant "to miss the mark," the way an arrow misses its target.

Q17 BE COMPASSIONATE AS YOUR Father is compassionate.

Do not judge, and you will not be judged.

Do not condemn, and you will not be condemned.

Forgive and you will be forgiven.

GIVE, AND THERE WILL be gifts for you. A full measure of grain, pressed down, shaken together and running over, will be poured into your lap; because the amount you measure out is the amount you will be given back. Q18

Q19 CAN ONE BLIND PERSON lead another? Won't they both fall into a ditch? The student is not superior to the teacher, but if students are well taught they will become like their teacher.

WHY DO YOU NOTICE the speck of sawdust in your brother's eye and not the wooden plank in your own? How can you say to your brother, "Let me take out the sawdust from your eye," when you cannot see the plank in your own? Q20

Hypocrite! Remove the plank from your own eye first; then you will see clearly enough to remove the sawdust from your brother's eye.

Who were the "hypocrites" Jesus criticizes here and in the New Testament Gospels? The Greek word was hypokrites, meaning an actor or orator, and in a derogatory sense, a pretender.

Q21 NO GOOD TREE PRODUCES rotten fruit and no bad tree produces good fruit. Each tree is known by its own fruit. People do not pick figs from thorn bushes, nor gather grapes from blackberry brambles. Good people draw what is good from the treasure of their hearts. Bad people produce what is bad from the evil within them. A person's words flow from what is treasured in the heart.

WHY DO YOU CALL me, "Lord, Lord" and not do what I say?

I will show you what the person who comes to me, hears what I have to say and acts accordingly is really like. That person is like someone building a house, who digs deeply and lays the foundation on bedrock. The rain pours down, the floods rise in a torrent, and the winds blow and beat upon the house, but it does not fall. It is built on rock.

But the one who listens and does nothing is like the person who builds a house on sand with no foundation. When the river bursts against it, it collapses immediately and is destroyed.

.3 AT THE TIME THAT Jesus entered Capernaum, a Roman officer there had a favorite servant who was sick and near death. Hearing about Jesus, the centurion sent some Jewish elders to ask him to come and heal his servant. They came to Jesus and pleaded urgently with him. "He deserves your help," they said. "He is a friend of our people; in fact, he is the one who built the synagogue."

Jesus was not very far from the house when the centurion approached him and said, "My servant is lying at home paralyzed and in great pain."

Jesus said to him, "I will come myself and cure him."

The centurion replied, "I don't deserve to have you in my house. But just say the word, and my servant will be healed. After all, I myself am under orders, and I have many soldiers under my command. I say to one, 'Go!' and he goes. I order another to come and he comes. And to my servant, 'Do this!' and he does it."

When Jesus heard this, he was amazed and said to the crowd following him, "I tell you, nowhere in Israel have I found such faith."

Then Jesus said to the centurion, "Go home now and everything will happen as you believed it would." At that moment, the servant was healed.

Could a centurion have been a friend to the Jews? In fact, many Greeks and Romans highly respected the Jews because of their unique worship of a single God. At least one ancient synagogue carried an inscription acknowledging the builder as a Gentile.

Q24 JOHN THE BAPTIST WAS in prison when he heard what Jesus was doing. He sent two of his own disciples to ask him, "Are you the one who is to come, or are we to wait for another?"

Jesus answered, "Go back and tell John what you hear and see: the blind see again, the lame walk, lepers are made clean, the deaf hear, the dead are raised to life and the poor are given good news. Blessed is the man who does not lose faith in me."

After John's disciples had departed, Jesus spoke to the crowds about John. "What did you go out to the desert to see? A reed shaken by the wind? No? Then what did you go out to see? A man dressed in fine clothes? Those who wear fine clothes live in luxury in royal palaces. But why did you go out? To see a prophet? Yes, I tell you—and much more than a prophet. He is the one about whom it is written:

'See, I send my messenger before you,
He will prepare the road ahead of you.'

"I tell you, of all the children born of women, no one is greater than John the Baptist; yet the least in the realm of God is greater than him."

UP UNTIL THE TIME of John the Baptist, Q25
we had the law of Moses and the words of the prophets. Since John arrived, the good news about God's realm has been announced. Now people everywhere are pushing to get in.

Q26 HOW SHOULD I DESCRIBE the people of this generation? What are they like?

They are like children who sit in the marketplace and call to one another:

"We played the flute for you and you didn't dance;

We sang sad songs and you would not weep."

For John the Baptist came, not eating bread, not drinking wine, and you said, "He is crazy."

Now the son of man comes, eating and drinking, and you say, "Just look at him, a glutton and a drunkard, a friend of tax collectors and outcasts."

But Wisdom is being proven right by all her children.

AS THEY WALKED ALONG the road, they met a man who said to Jesus, "I will follow you wherever you go." Jesus answered, "Foxes have dens and birds have nests, but the son of man has nowhere to rest his head." Q27

To another he said, "Follow me." But that person replied, "Let me go and bury my father first." Jesus answered, "Let the dead bury their dead. Your duty is to go and spread the news of the realm of God."

Another person said, "I will follow you, but first let me go and say good-bye to my family." Jesus said to him, "No one who puts a hand on the plough and continues to look at what was left behind is suited for the realm of God."

One of the most problematic phrases in the Bible is "the kingdom of God" (translated here as "the realm of God"). The Aramaic and Hebrew words of Jesus did not imply a territory or domain. Instead, they referred to a power that is coming to be. Far from an earthly empire, the "kingdom of God" sometimes lies hidden and at other times appears in mysterious ways—as in the form of a mustard seed.

Q28 ALTHOUGH THE CROP IS abundant, there are few workers to harvest it, so ask the owner to send more laborers out into the fields. Get going, but remember, I am sending you out like lambs among wolves.

DON'T ACQUIRE GOLD, SILVER or copper. Q29
Carry no purse, no knapsack, no sandals. Don't bring a second tunic or a staff. Don't stop to greet people along the way.

The knapsack and the staff (used as a walking stick and to ward off wild animals) were characteristic symbols of wandering Cynic philosophers. Jesus may be distinguishing his followers from these itinerants, who also took a vow of poverty.

Q30 WHENEVER YOU ENTER SOMEONE'S home, let your first words be, "Peace to this house!" If a person who loves peace lives there, they will accept your blessing. If not, your words will come back to you. Stay in this house, taking what food and drink they offer, for the laborer deserves his reward. Do not keep moving from house to house. When you enter a town and the people welcome you, eat the food they provide. Heal the sick who are there. Say to the people of the town, "The realm of God is at your door."

IF YOU ENTER A town and they do not welcome you, go out into its streets and say, "We wipe off the very dust of your town that clings to our feet, and leave it with you. Yet be sure of this: the realm of God is very near." Q31

I tell you, on that day Sodom and Gomorrah will be better off than that town.

Beware, Chorazin! Take heed, Bethsaida! If Tyre and Sidon had seen the miracles performed in your midst, they would have changed their ways long ago, sitting in sackcloth and ashes. It will not go as hard with Tyre and Sidon at the judgment as with you. As for you, Capernaum, do you think you will be exalted to the heavens? No, you shall go crashing down among the dead!

Anyone who listens to you listens to me. Whoever rejects you rejects me, and those who reject me reject the one who sent me.

The towns of Chorazin and Bethsaida were near Capernaum, the fishing village on the Sea of Galilee that was the center of Jesus' activity. He probably shocked his followers by favoring the notoriously pagan centers of Tyre and Sidon over their own homeland. These Mediterranean cities were infamous in the Old Testament as the home of the idol-worshiping Queen Jezebel.

Q32 AT THIS TIME, JESUS said, "I thank you, Father, for hiding these things from the wise and the clever and revealing them to the childlike. This is the way you want it. Everything has been put in my hand by my father. No one knows who the son is except the father, and who the father is except the son, and anyone to whom the son chooses to reveal him."

WHEN JESUS WAS ALONE with his disciples, Q33
he turned to them and said, "Fortunate are the eyes that see what you are seeing. Many prophets and kings wished to see what you now see and never saw it, longed to hear what you now hear and never heard it."

Q34 ONE DAY IT HAPPENED that Jesus was praying in a particular place. When he finished, one of his disciples said, "Lord, teach us how to pray just as John the Baptist taught his disciples."

He responded, "Say this when you pray:

'Father, may your name be honored;
may your reign begin.

Grant us the food we need for each day.

Forgive our failures,
for we forgive everyone who fails us.

And do not put us to the test.' "

Known to Protestants as the Lord's Prayer and to Catholics as the Our Father, this simple prayer includes a single word that proclaims a radically new relationship between humankind and God. Throughout the Old Testament, the names for God imply power and remoteness. Here Jesus addresses God as "Abba," a warm and informal term for Father that is akin to our word Papa.

ASK AND IT'LL BE given to you. Search and you will find. Knock and the door will be opened for you. For everyone who asks receives, and everyone who searches finds, and for those who knock, the door is opened. Q35

Q36 WHO AMONG YOU WOULD hand his son a stone when he has asked you for bread? Who would hand him a snake when it's fish he's asking for? If you, who are imperfect, know how to give good things to your child, how much more will your heavenly Father give to you when you ask.

THEY BROUGHT A MAN who was blind and Q37
mute and who was possessed by a demon to Jesus. He cured the man so that he could speak and see.

The crowds were astonished. But some of them said, "He is in league with Beelzebul, the chief of the evil spirits."

But Jesus answered them, "If it is by the power of Beelzebul that I cast out demons, by whose power do your own people cast them out? If I rely on the help of the chief of the demons to cast out demons, then Beelzebul's own house is divided against itself. Every kingdom divided against itself will be destroyed, and a house divided in two will collapse. So if Satan's house is divided, how can his kingdom survive?

"But if it is by the finger of God that I cast out demons, then the reign of God has arrived!"

Jesus was not the only healer in the land. Unlike other healers of the day, however, he used no charms, incantations or paraphernalia, but relied upon the power inherent in "the finger of God."

Q38 ANYONE WHO IS NOT with me is against me. Whoever does not help me gather scatters.

WHEN AN UNCLEAN SPIRIT goes out of a person, it wanders through waterless country looking for a place to rest. Not finding one it says, "I will go back to the home I came from." But on arrival, finding it swept and tidied, it then goes off and brings seven other spirits more wicked than itself, and they go in and set up house there, so that the person ends up by being worse than before. Q39

In Jewish folklore, demons and evil spirits could be destroyed by water, so they roamed the desert looking for a resting place.

Q40 As Jesus was speaking, a woman in the crowd raised her voice and said, "Blessed is the womb that gave birth to you and the breasts that nursed you."

He replied, "Blessed rather are those who hear the word of God and observe it."

WITH THE CROWDS SWARMING around him, Q41
Jesus addressed the people directly, "You are an imperfect generation! You demand a sign, but none will be given except the sign of Jonah. Just as Jonah was a symbol for the people of Nineveh, so will the son of man be for today's generation.

"The Queen of Sheba traveled from the ends of the earth to hear the wisdom of Solomon. Today, something greater than Solomon is here. The people of Nineveh heard the preaching of Jonah and changed their ways. But now, something greater than Jonah is here.

"At the judgment, both the Queen of Sheba and the Ninevites will condemn this generation."

In the Old Testament, the Queen of Sheba came from Ethiopia to meet King Solomon and "test him with hard questions." Like the people of Nineveh mentioned in this passage, she was a Gentile. So it is interesting to note that after hearing Solomon's responses, she went away convinced of his wisdom.

Q42 NO ONE LIGHTS A lamp and puts it under a bushel basket. They put it on a stand so that everyone can see the light. Your eye is the lamp of your body. When your eye is clear, your entire body fills with light. But if your eye becomes clouded, your body is in darkness. Be careful that your light never fades into darkness.

Lamps in first-century Galilee were small terra-cotta lanterns that burned oil and were often the only source of light inside the windowless houses of the region.

BEWARE, YOU WHO CALL yourselves perfect in your obedience to the law. You pay the tax on mint, dill and cumin, but you ignore justice, mercy and honesty. You should practice these things first. Q43

You wash the outside of your cups and plates, but inside you are filled with thoughts of greed and theft. Didn't the one who made the outside make the inside too? Wash the inside of the cup and it will all be clean.

The ritual washing of kitchen utensils was a common practice among devout Jewish groups. Jesus' failure to follow these cleanliness codes was seen as a sign of his rebelliousness against the religious establishment.

Q44 You who claim to be the most devout are hopeless! You love sitting in the front row of the synagogue and having people bow down to you in public. You are like whitewashed tombs—beautiful on the surface, but filled with death and decay.

Beware to those who load people down with the crushing burden of laws and regulations but do nothing to help them. You have taken away the key of knowledge, but instead of unlocking the door, you have blocked the way for those trying to enter.

You erect monuments to prophets who were murdered by your ancestors. They did the killing, you built the tombs.

That's why the Wisdom of God said, "I will send them prophets and messengers. Some they will kill, others they will persecute. This generation will have to answer for the blood of every prophet shed since the beginning of the world, from Abel to Zechariah."

THERE IS NOTHING COVERED up now that will not be exposed. Nothing is secret that will not be revealed. Every secret you've kept will become known. What you have whispered in hidden places will be shouted from the housetops. Q45

Q46 DO NOT FEAR THOSE who kill the body but cannot kill the soul. Instead, you should respect the one who holds in his hands both your body and your soul. What does a sparrow cost? A few pennies? Yet not a single little bird is forgotten by God. And you? God's care extends to every hair on your head. You are worth more than a flock of sparrows.

Sold in the village markets of Galilee, sparrows, though tiny, were cheap and plentiful, and served as a common food for the poor.

EVERYONE WHO ACKNOWLEDGES ME in public will be celebrated by the angels. 047

Q48 WHOEVER REJECTS ME BEFORE others will be disowned by the angels. Anyone who speaks against the son of man will be forgiven, but there is no forgiveness for those who attack the Holy Spirit.

When you are dragged into court and forced to appear before judges because of your beliefs, don't worry about how to defend yourself or what to say. The words will come to you from the Holy Spirit when you need them.

SOMEONE IN THE CROWD said to him, Q49
"Teacher, tell my brother to share the family inheritance with me."

Jesus responded, "Friend, who made me a judge?"

Q50 THERE WAS ONCE A rich man whose lands yielded a good harvest. He thought to himself, "What should I do? I don't have enough room to store my crops. I know, I'll tear down my barns and build bigger ones so that I can keep all my grain in them. Then I will say to myself, 'I have enough to last me for years. I can take it easy, eat, drink and have a good time.' "

But God said to him, "You fool! This very night you may die. Then who will own this hoard of yours?" So it is with those who pile up possessions but remain poor in the treasures of the spirit.

JESUS SPOKE TO HIS disciples: "Don't be anxious about your life. Don't worry about getting enough food or having clothes to wear. Life means more than food and the body is more than clothing. Look at the ravens. They don't plant seeds or gather a harvest. They have neither storehouses nor barns. Yet God feeds them. Aren't you more important than birds? Can any of you, for all your worrying, add a single moment to your life? If worry can't change the smallest thing, then why be anxious about the rest?" Q51

Jesus probably chose the raven here to sharpen his point. Roman naturalists like Pliny the Elder thought that these birds were so careless they sometimes forgot to return to their nests! And under Jewish law, ravens were considered unclean. Many rabbis even believed that mentioning the raven in a prayer was blasphemous.

Q52 LOOK AT THE LILIES that grow wild in the fields. They don't weave clothes for themselves. But I tell you, even King Solomon in all his splendor was not dressed as beautifully as these flowers. If that is how God clothes the grasses, which are green today and burned in the sun tomorrow, how much more will God provide for you. How little faith you have!

A master of the spoken word, Jesus often used puns and poetic devices in his speech. Here, in describing the weaving of clothes, he uses the rhyming Aramaic words amal and azal.

DON'T BE BLINDED BY the pursuit of food, clothing and possessions. Stop worrying about these things. Only those who lack spirit and soul pursue them. You have a Father who knows what you need. Set your heart on God and these other things will be given to you. Q53

Q54 DON'T PILE UP YOUR treasures here on earth. They will be destroyed by moths and rust and stolen by thieves. Store your riches in heaven where moths and rust are powerless and thieves cannot break in. Wherever your treasure is, your heart will also be.

IF THE OWNER OF a house knows when a thief is coming, he will be on guard and not let anyone break into the house. You too must be prepared—the son of man will arrive when you least expect him. Q55

Ancient Jews believed that breaking through a doorway brought bad luck, even to a thief. So the words Jesus uses here literally mean breaking through thick walls made of mud or clay bricks.

Q56 WHEN THE OWNER OF an estate wants a manager who can be trusted with all his goods, someone who will make sure the staff is cared for and fed, whom will he put in charge? A trusty and sensible supervisor. Congratulations to that person if he proves faithful and is hard at work when the owner comes home. In that case, the owner will give him a share in all his property. But if the manager says to himself, "The owner is not coming back for a long time," and begins abusing the workers and feasting and getting drunk, the owner may return unexpectedly. Instead of receiving a reward, the manager will be cut off and will share the fate of the unfaithful.

DO YOU SUPPOSE THAT I am here to bring peace? No, I have come to bring the sword of division. My message will divide father and son, mother and daughter, mother-in-law and daughter-in-law. Q57

Those who prefer their father or mother to me are not deserving. Nor are those who prefer their sons and daughters.

Unless you carry your own cross and follow me, you are not worthy.

The Romans crucified two thousand Jews during the rebellion that followed King Herod the Great's death in 4 B.C.E., so Jesus' followers were well acquainted with crucifixion even before his death. It was common practice in these executions to have the condemned person carry his own cross to the place of crucifixion.

Q58 THOSE WHO GRASP AND clutch at self will lose it. Those who let go of self and follow me will find it.

WHEN YOU SEE CLOUDS in the western sky, you say, "It's going to rain." And it does! When the wind blows from the south, you predict scorching weather. And it comes! You know the lay of the land and can read the face of the sky. So why can't you interpret the here and now? Q59

A vital aspect of the Lost Gospel Q is its earthiness. Whereas the book's message is universal, the imagery is personal and local. Here Jesus refers to the rain clouds that entered Galilee from the Mediterranean Sea to the west and the hot winds that swept in from the Negev Desert in the south.

Q60 WHY CAN'T YOU JUDGE for yourselves what is right? When you are headed for court with an opponent, try to settle the case on the way and make peace with him. Otherwise he will call you before the judge, who may turn you over to the jailer. Then you may not get out of jail until you've paid your last penny.

WHAT IS THE REALM of God like? How can I describe it to you? It is like a tiny mustard seed that someone tosses into a garden. It grows into a tree and birds nest in its branches. Q61

For centuries, Jewish prophets compared the realm of God to the famed cedars of Lebanon, which were used to build the temple of Solomon in Jerusalem. So Jesus is shocking his audience by likening it to a tiny mustard seed, which grew into a scraggly plant that most farmers considered a weed.

Q62 TO WHAT SHALL I compare the realm of God? It is like yeast that a woman takes and mixes with three cups of flour until it all rises.

ENTER BY THE NARROW gate. The path that Q63
leads to destruction is wide and easy. Many follow it. But the narrow gate and hard road lead to life. Few discover it.

Q64 I PREDICT THAT PEOPLE will come from east and west, and north and south to sit with Abraham, Isaac and Jacob at a great banquet in the realm of heaven. Those who think the realm of God belongs to them will be thrown out into the dark where they will cry tears of bitter regret.

THE LAST WILL BE first and the first will be last. φ65

Q66 JERUSALEM, O JERUSALEM, YOU are a city that kills the prophets and stones those who are sent to you. How often I have wanted to gather your children as a hen gathers her chicks under her wings. But you have not let me. See, your house will be abandoned and left in ruins. You will not see me again until you say, "Blessed is the one who comes in the name of the Lord."

There is a hidden irony when Jesus calls Jerusalem a "city that kills." Its name actually derives from the Hebrew word "shalom," which implies the absence of strife and hostility. Jerusalem literally means "city of peace."

THOSE WHO PRAISE THEMSELVES will be humbled. Those who humble themselves will be praised. Q67

968 A MAN ONCE GAVE a great banquet and invited many guests. As the dinner hour approached, he sent a servant to tell them, "Come, everything is ready now." One by one, they started making excuses. The first guest told the servant, "I'm sorry but I just bought a piece of land and have to go see it."

Another guest said, "You'll have to excuse me, I'm on my way to take a look at five pairs of oxen that I've purchased."

A third guest explained, "I just got married and I can't come."

The servant returned to tell the host about all these excuses.

In a fit of anger, the man shouted, "Go out right now into the streets and alleys and invite the poor, the crippled, the blind and the lame."

Soon, the servant reported back, "I've carried out your orders, but there is still room."

"Then go farther out to the roads and country lanes," the man responded, "and lead people back until my house is filled. But not one of those original guests will share this feast."

To the cultures of the Middle East, sharing a meal signified much more than simply eating together. To invite a person to dinner was to honor them; and very strict Jewish rules dictated who was a suitable guest. Jesus is turning this tradition upside down by inviting the homeless to share a meal while excluding the wealthy.

φ69 IF YOU LOVE YOUR father and mother, or your son and daughter, more than me, you cannot follow me. Unless you take up your cross and let go of all you possess, you cannot truly follow me.

YOU ARE THE SALT of the earth. But if salt loses Q70
its taste, it can never be salty again. It will be worthless. It won't even be fit for the manure pile.

Mined along the Dead Sea, the saltiest body of water in the world, salt was a vital ingredient in the daily and spiritual life of the ancient world. Homer and Plato said it was "beloved of the gods," and Plutarch claimed that it was the spice of wit and conversation. To the Jews of the Old Testament, eating salt together was a sign of loyalty and purity.

Q71 SUPPOSE SOMEONE HAS A hundred sheep and one of them strays. Won't he leave the other ninety-nine on the hillside and search for the one that wandered away? When he finds it, he'll lift the sheep onto his shoulders in joy. Then, coming home, he'll call out to his friends and neighbors, "Let's celebrate! I've found the sheep that was lost."

It was a rare lamb that was lost in first-century Galilee. Each shepherd had a unique whistle known only to his flock. If two flocks became hopelessly intermixed at a watering spot, the herder needed simply to whistle softly for his flock to immediately part from the other sheep and follow him.

IF A WOMAN HAS ten silver coins, what will she do if she loses one? She'll light a lamp, sweep the house and search carefully. When she finds it, she will call her friends and neighbors and say to them, "Let's celebrate! I've found the coin that was lost." Q72

Made of mud and covered by thatched roofs, houses in Galilee had rough dirt floors and lacked even a single window. So losing a silver coin was no small matter.

Q73 NO ONE CAN SERVE two masters. You will either hate the first and love the second or treat one with respect and the other with scorn. You can not serve both God and money.

The Gospel of Thomas, the Q-like manuscript discovered in Egypt in 1945, includes a variation on this problem of serving two masters. "One cannot mount two horses," it explains, "or pull back two strings on a bow."

As LONG AS HEAVEN and earth endure, not one letter, not a single dot of the Law, will disappear. Q74

Q75 ANYONE WHO DIVORCES HIS wife and remarries commits adultery. So does a man who marries a divorced woman.

OBSTACLES TO FAITH ARE sure to arise, but beware to the one who creates them. It would be better for that person to be thrown into the sea with a millstone tied around the neck than for that person to mislead one of my followers. Q76

Q77 JESUS EXPLAINED TO HIS disciples, "If a companion does something wrong to you, go to the person and point this out. But do it privately. If your friend listens and says, 'I'm sorry,' forgive and your bond will be strengthened."

"But how often must I forgive the same person?" asked one of his disciples. "Seven times?"

Jesus answered, "Not just seven times, but seventy-seven times."

EVEN IF YOUR FAITH is no bigger than a mustard seed, you can say to this mountain, "Move!" and it will move. Nothing will be impossible for you. Q78

Q79 JESUS WAS ASKED, "WHEN will the kingdom of God arrive?"

He replied, "You won't be able see the kingdom of God when it comes. People won't be able to say 'it's here' or 'it's over there.'

"The kingdom of God is among you."

A TIME WILL COME when you will long to see the son of man, but you'll see nothing. There will be those who will say, "Look over there" or "Look right here." But don't go searching! Stay right where you are. Because the son of man will come like lightning flashing from one end of the sky to the other. Q80

It will be just like it was in the days of Noah. People ate, drank, got married and went on with their lives right up until the day that Noah climbed aboard the ark. Then the flood came and destroyed them. That's how it will be when the son of man is revealed.

If two people are sleeping, one will be taken, the other left. If two women are grinding grain at the mill, one will be taken, the other will be left.

Q81 A NOBLEMAN ONCE WENT off to a distant land to become king. Just before he left, he called together his ten most trusted servants and gave each of them ten silver coins. "See what you can earn with this money while I am gone," he instructed them.

His fellow citizens, however, hated him and sent a delegation saying, "We don't want this man to rule over us!"

Nevertheless, he received the kingship and returned home. He summoned the servants to find out what each one had done with the money.

The first one said, "I've turned the ten coins into one hundred!"

"Excellent," the new king replied. "Because you've proven trustworthy in this small matter, I'm going to put you in charge of ten towns."

The second one reported, "I've earned five times what you gave me."

"Then you'll be in charge of five towns," replied the king.

Another servant stepped forward and said, "Sir, here are your coins. I kept them wrapped in a handkerchief because you're a hard man and I'm afraid of you. You always try to get something for nothing. You reap where you do not sow."

"Listen to what you're saying!" the king said. "You're trapped by your own words. You say that I'm a difficult man, that I try to get something for nothing. If that's true, why didn't you do something with the money to make a profit? You've disobeyed me."

Turning to the others, he said, "Take the silver coins from him and give them to the fellow who turned ten coins into one hundred."

"But sir!" they protested. "He already has a hundred coins."

"Yes," the king replied, "and to the person who has something, more will be given and that person will have an abundance. The person who has nothing of real value will lose even what he thinks he has."

Q82 JESUS SAID TO HIS followers, "You have stayed close to me through all of my trials. You will eat and drink with me in the realm of God."

A Note on the Translation

Translation is risky business. William Tyndale, the great English translator, was executed by strangulation for the heretical act of rendering the Latin Bible into English. Just ten years earlier, the Bishop of London held a public burning of English-language Bibles that had been smuggled in from new printing presses on the continent.

That was during the 1500s. By early the next century, the situation had improved markedly. In fact, when King James II mandated a group of almost fifty British scholars to produce a new edition of the Bible, he cautioned them not to work in a vacuum, but to review existing translations. As a result, the King James Bible, which many people look upon as the crowning achievement of English prose, is hardly original. It depends in large part on earlier translations.

Today, with two dozen massively researched translations and revisions of the Gospels produced during the last quarter century alone, we also have avoided working in a vacuum. We have drawn on the New English Bible, Jerusalem Bible, Today's English Version, New Revised Standard Version and the New American Standard as well as the experiments in prose undertaken by individual translators such as James Moffat, Ronald Knox, Edgar Goodspeed and J. B. Phillips.

This edition of the Lost Gospel Q does not pretend to be *the* scholarly version. In fact, many scholars would call our rendering a "paraphrase" since we have followed the principle of "dynamic equivalence" in producing the text. This modern style of translation seeks to re-create a text in contemporary language by focusing on sentences, paragraphs and overall meaning rather than seeking a word-for-word equivalence. Our goal has been to rebuild the scattered fragments of the Lost Gospel Q in a fashion that gives form and meaning to the resulting structure. Q is, after all, a diamond in the rough—brilliant, multifaceted and sharp—but lacking in symmetry and polish.

We are extremely grateful to the guiding hand of Marcus Borg, our consulting editor, whose sensitivity to both the meaning of the original text and the beauty of the language has helped direct our interpretation. Together with Dr. Borg, we believe that the Lost Gospel Q is a powerful and important book both for spiritual seekers and those in search of the historical Jesus.

—Mark Powelson and Ray Riegert, Editors

Q PARALLELS

Q SAYING	MATTHEW	LUKE
1	3:1–3	3:2b–4
2	3:5–10	3:7–11
3		3:12–14
4	3:11–12	3:16–17
5	3:13, 16–17	3:21b–22
6	4:1–4	4:1–4
7	4:5–7	4:9–12
8	4:8–11	4:5–8, 13
9	5:1–2, 3, 6	6:12, 17, 20–21
10	5:6; 5:4	6:21
11	5:5	
12	5:7–9	
13	5:11–12	6:22–23
14	5:44, 46	6:27–28
15	5:39b–42	6:29–30
16	7:12; 5:46–47	6:31–33, 35b
17	5:48	6:36
18	7:1–2	6:38
19	15:14; 10:24–25	6:39–40
20	7:3–5	6:41–42
21	7:16–20; 12:35	6:43–45
22	7:21–27	6:46–49
23	8:5–13	7:1b–10
24	11:2–11	7:18–20, 22–28
25	11:12–13	16:16
26	11:16–19	7:31–35
27	8:19–22	9:57–60
28	10:16; 9:37	10:2–3
29	10:9–10	9:3; 10:4
30	10:11–12	10:5–9
31	10:40, 11:21–23	10:10–12, 13–16
32	11:25–27	10:21–22
33	13:16–17	10:23–24
34	6:9–13	11:1–4
35	7:7–8	11:9–11
36	7:9–11	11:11–13
37	12:22–28	11:14–20
38	12:30	11:23
39	12:43–45	11:24–26
40		11:27–28
41	12:38–42	11:16, 29–32

Q SAYING	MATTHEW	LUKE
42	5:15, 16:22–23	11:33–36
43	23:23, 26	11:39–42
44	23:6–7, 29–35	11:43–51
45	10:26–27	12:2–3
46	10:28–31	12:4–7
47	10:32	12:8
48	10:19–20; 12:32	12:9–12
49		12:13–14
50		12:16–21
51	6:25–27	12:22–26
52	6:28–30	12:27–28
53	6:31–33	12:29–31
54	6:19–21	12:33–34
55	24:42–44	12:39–40
56	24:45–51	12:42–46
57	10:34–36	12:51–53
58	10:39	17:33
59	16:2–3	12:54–56
60	5:25–26	12:57–59
61	13:31–32	13:18–19
62	13:33	13:20–21
63	7:13–14	13:24
64	8:11–12	13:28–29
65	20:16	13:30
66	23:37–39	13:34–35
67	23:12	14:11
68	22:1–10	14:16–24
69	10:37–38	14:26–27
70	5:13	14:34–35
71	18:12–13	15:4–7
72		15:8–10
73	6:24	16:13
74	5:18	16:17
75	5:32	16:18
76	18:6–7	17:1–2
77	18:15, 21–22	17:3–4
78	17:20	17:6
79		17:20–21
80	24:26, 37–41	17:22–26, 34
81	25:14–30	19:12–23
82	19:28	22:28–30

Bibliography

Aaland, Kurt, ed. *Synopsis of the Four Gospels*. 10th ed. Stuttgart: German Bible Society, 1993.

Albright, W. F. and Mann, C. S. *Matthew: A New Translation with Introduction and Commentary*. New York: Anchor Doubleday, 1971.

Beare, Francis Wright. *The Earliest Records of Jesus: A Companion to the Synopsis of the First Three Gospels, by Albert Huck*. New York: Abingdon Press, 1962.

Black, Matthew. *An Aramaic Approach to the Gospels and Acts*. 3d ed. Oxford: Oxford University Press, 1967.

Catchpole, David R. *The Quest for Q*. Edinburgh: T&T Clark, 1993.

Charlesworth, James H., ed. *Jesus and the Dead Sea Scrolls*. New York: Anchor Doubleday, 1992.

Crossan, John Dominic. *In Fragments: The Aphorisms of Jesus*. San Francisco: Harper & Row, 1983.

_________, ed. *Sayings Parallels: A Workbook for the Jesus Tradition*. Philadelphia: Fortress Press, 1986.

Davies, W. D., and Allison, Dale C., Jr. *The Gospel According to Saint Matthew: A Critical and Exegetical Commentary*. 2 vols. Edinburgh: T & T Clark, 1991.

Edwards, Richard A. *A Theology of Q: Eschatology, Prophecy, and Wisdom*. Philadelphia: Fortress Press, 1976.

Fitzmyer, Joseph A. *The Gospel According to Luke*. 2 vols. New York: Anchor Doubleday, 1981.

Guelich, Robert. *The Sermon on the Mount: A Foundation for Understanding*. Dallas: Word Publishing, 1982.

Harnack, Adolf von. *The Sayings of Jesus: The Second Source of St. Matthew and St. Luke*. New York: G. P. Putnam, 1908.

Havener, Ivan. *Q: The Sayings of Jesus*. Wilmington, Delaware: M. Glazier, 1987.

Horsley, Richard A. *Sociology and the Jesus Movement*. 2d ed. New York: Continuum, 1994.

Jacobson, Arland Dean. *The First Gospel: An Introduction to Q*. Sonoma, California: Polebridge Press, 1991.

Jeremias, Joachim. *Jerusalem in the Time of Jesus*. Philadelphia: Fortress Press, 1969.

__________. *The Parables of Jesus*. 2d U.S. ed. New York: Charles Scribner's Sons, 1963.

Kloppenborg, John S. *The Formation of Q: Trajectories in Ancient Wisdom Collections*. Philadelphia: Fortress Press, 1987.

__________. *Q Parallels: Synopsis, Critical Notes, & Concordance*. Sonoma, California: Polebridge Press, 1988.

__________. *Q-Thomas Reader*. Sonoma, California: Polebridge Press, 1990.

__________, ed. *The Shape of Q: Signal Essays on the Sayings Gospel*. Minneapolis: Fortress Press, 1994.

Mack, Burton. *The Lost Gospel: The Book of Q & Christian Origins*. San Francisco: Harper San Francisco, 1993.

__________. *Who Wrote the New Testament?: The Making of the Christian Myth*. San Francisco: Harper San Francisco, 1995.

Manson, T. W. *The Sayings of Jesus*. 2d ed. London: SCM Press, 1948.

Marshall, I. Howard. *Commentary on Luke: A Commentary on the Greek Text*. Grand Rapids: William Eerdmans Publishing, 1978.

Meier, John P. *A Marginal Jew: Rethinking the Historical Jesus*. 2 vols. New York: Anchor Doubleday, 1991, 1994.

Patterson, Stephen J. *The Gospel of Thomas and Jesus*. Sonoma, California: Polebridge Press, 1991.

Piper, Ronald A. *Wisdom in the Q-Tradition: The Aphoristic Teaching of Jesus*. Cambridge; New York: Cambridge University Press, 1989.

Robinson, James. " 'Logoi Sophon': On the *Gattung* of Q." In James Robinson and Helmut Koester (eds.), *Trajectories through Early Christianity*. Philadelphia: Fortress Press, 1971.

Rousseau, John J. and Arav, Rami. *Jesus and His World*. Minneapolis: Augsburg Fortress Press, 1995.

Theissen, Gerd (John Bowden, trans.). *Sociology of Early Palestinian Christianity*. Philadelphia: Fortress Press, 1978.

Vaage, Leif E. *Galilean Upstarts: Jesus' First Followers According to Q*. Valley Forge, Pennsylvania: Trinity Press International, 1994.

MARCUS BORG is "a leading figure among the new generation of Jesus scholars," according to the *New York Times*. With a Ph.D. from Oxford, he is the author of several books, including *The God We Never Knew* and *Jesus: A New Vision*. Dr. Borg is a professor of religion at Oregon State University.

THOMAS MOORE is the author of *Care of the Soul*, the *New York Times* bestseller. His most recently published work is *Original Self*. Dr. Moore lived for twelve years as a Catholic monk and received his Ph.D. in religious studies from Syracuse University.

MARK POWELSON is a writer and editor who has written on spirituality and New Testament interpretation. Currently a student of religion at the Graduate Theological Union in Berkeley, California, he is also member of the Society of Biblical Literature.

RAY RIEGERT has been an editor and publisher for twenty years. A member of the American Academy of Religion and the Society of Biblical Literature, he is the co-author of *The Gospel of Thomas* and an editor of *Jesus and Buddha: The Parallel Sayings*.